Listen to me, Ya!

A Satire by Dr. Mohan G. Shenoy

Adyar Gopal Parivar Publications,

Bangalore, India.

Listen to me, Ya! is an out of the box satire written for readers who wish to listen to every person that presents his side of the subject. Almost every topic about which there are different views is discussed in a question and answer format. It reads like a conversation between two individuals.

First Edition   June 2017

Sale price   ₹500 in India and USD 8 in other countries.

D. T. P.   Mohan G. Shenoy

Print   Createspace, U. S. A.

Country of Publication   India

Dedication   To the Youth of India and the world.

Genre   Satirical Fiction.

Cover design   Dorko

———————————

DESCRIPTION

In this book there are social and some political, regional, religious and linguistic issues discussed. It is written in the form of conversation between an elderly person and a youngster. The youngsters are eager to know how to gain health, wealth, fame and happiness in life. The aged person may not really be better informed but he or she has survived the complex path of life and ought to have learnt from life's experiences. What are his or her explanations of them?

This book is for those readers who have a lot of free time and consider reading books as a sport they like. The habit of reading books is not present in all educated people. There are many books that will not contain anything that some people consider to be of use to them. An author always writes those things that he or she considers as worthy of reading. But the reader will decide what is to be read and what is really useful. So long as there are facilities available to print and publish books, there will be authors who write them and sportive persons who read them.

To find what the reader wishes to read, there is a list of keywords given here. A reader might stop going further once he or she finds nothing that is of interest to him or her. But there is one or other subject in this book that will interest a particular reader. Yet, only those who have developed interest in common tenets of life will find something interesting and not those who are looking for specific information pertaining to their query.

I wish the readers a joyful and happy reading.

Dr. Mohan G. Shenoy,
Author

KEYWORDS

1 to 9
12th class, 22
14-yr old, 20
8th class, 19
9th class, 21

A and B
accident, 13
act deaf, 38
adult content, 63
Ancient Indians, 40
Animals, 50
Anti-smoking lobby, 32
Ayurveda, 44
Ayush, 44
behaviour, 50
bribes, 11

C and D
capitalist, 7
career, 20, 28
child labour, 26
cigarette, 33
Cleanliness, 60
companion, 48, 67
conscience, 5
Cost of medical care, 45
Death, 67
Democracy, 60
divine attributes, 44
dropouts, 30

E and F
earth, 66
Economics, 54
Education, 17
    Structure of, 18
enjoy life, 58
expenses, 58
fatal disease, 52
female workers, 12
Fire hazard, 33
food habits, 4
forgetfulness, 47
future, 67

G and H
giveaway, 41
gods, 15
governance, 63
healthcare, 46
Hindu Shastras, 68
History, 4
honesty, 6

I, K and L
income tax, 13
India, 18
Internet, 42
Konkani, 43
Language, 62
laziness, 49
lifestyle, 3

M
marriage, 24
Matric, 23
Media, 39
Medicine, 43
memory, 47
mind, 16
mobile phone, 61
money, 40
mothers, 35
mythological stories, 53

N, O, P and Q
newspapers, 53
Overindulgence, 65
personality, 6
politician, 42
prayers, 15
Pre-Vocation Course, 30
quacks, 8
quote, 60

R
Red Light Areas, 66
Renunciation, 48
retired life, 52

S and T
S. S. L. C. (Matric), 23
scholars, 2
school dropouts, 28
School Leaving, 19
science, 5

Secularism, 64
Secure borders, 60
self-punishment, 16
smiling, 51
smoking, 32
Soul, 68
spare time, 61
Spoken law, 31
Success, 65
Sun, 37
survival
    policy of, 51
thoughts, 66
tiger, 50
tobacco, 32
torture, 65

V, U, W, X, Y, Z.
Truth, 62
vested interests, 39
Votership, 61
wealth, 56
Welfare benefits, 55
wife, 36, 56
wild animals, 52
woman, 35
workers, 11
worth, 59
Yajna, 15
Yoga, 3

A SAMPLE

"History keeps repeating and has neither beginning nor end. Ancient Indians avoided recording dates to refrain from writing personal taints."

"I was like any other adolescent, later a young man was a prey to vices but I found smoking cigarettes or chewing paan are the least harmful."

"If there was ban on smoking in 1950-60s, like it is now, then I might have taken up some other vice such as drugs, alcohol, etc., as is now."

"I found drinking 4 cups of coffee or tea with/without sugar is worse for health than smoking ten cigarettes a day but all of them help man. Smokers are peace loving and not troublemakers and designating smoking areas in cities, airports, bus and railway stations makes us all a happy lot."

"Unexpected instant income puzzles my mind," said Ya. Ya was paid bonus of over ten thousand rupees for the year by his employer. "Lumpsum income ultimately makes me happy because I can now reset my priorities to a beneficial higher level. I am elated when I do any work that fulfils my aspirations even if my work isn't appreciated by my own relatives, friends or acquaintances."

Listen to me, Ya!

1.

Movan was old enough to be the grandfather of Ya. Ya, also known as Yarinna, was in fact not the grandson of Movan but only an acquaintance. They grew fond of each other when they met just a few months ago in the park where Movan comes to stroll in the mornings and evenings. They were always seen sitting together on the park bench. Ya was a young man just graduated from the University. He had so many questions in his mind for which he was seeking answers. Most of the people he asked the questions either could not answer them to his liking or Ya did not accept their answers.

Today, Ya and Movan came early to the park and sat on the same bench on which they sat the previous day. Movan started the conversation.

"What bothers you today, Ya?" Said he. "You know, by talking to you I get to think about the subject more deeply and refresh my knowledge about them. There are many subjects about which opinions have been expressed by scholars and thinkers throughout past centuries. Their ideas and opinions were relevant to their time and to the then prevalent knowledge."

Ya listened to Movan attentively.

Movan continued. "There have been since then so many advances in our civilization and we will be foolish if we stick to old systems and practices. We learn from books and other records but we ourselves did not experience them."

"Sir, do you think the information in the books are wrong?" Ya asked.

"They are not wrong until they are so proved by our modern findings and discoveries," replied Movan. "We first learn the language of the books in which they were written and understand correctly the meaning. The authors wanted to convey. It is easy to misinterpret old manuscripts and derive affirmation of our declared beliefs and concepts."

"We form an opinion and get support from ancient writings of which we give our own interpretation. We modify our interpretations to suit our declared beliefs and concepts," said Ya and asked, "Is that what you are saying?"

"Yes, Ya!" said Movan. "We quote from writings of well-known scholars in support of what we think and write," said Movan. "We want people to take it for granted that those quotes from past scholars affirm correctness of our own beliefs."

"In India, quoting western scholars has been in practice by teachers in our schools, colleges and in higher institutions of learning," said Movan. "It is assumed that we follow what those scholars with British or American names are saying. We do not raise any doubts over them."

"What the western scholars said suited the economic and social conditions then prevailed," intervened Ya. "In India the economic, social and political environment might not compare well with them."

"Yes. That is what I am saying," said Movan. "We got to create our own database for use by us in every sphere of life. We should draw information from every source, western, eastern, and central and prepare a modern book of knowledge for our use consistent with the local conditions."

Movan took out a small plastic bottle from the cloth bag he had brought with him. It was a water bottle from which Movan drank some water. At this, Ya also pulled out the water bottle he had in his briefcase and drank some water out of it. A few walkers that went past this pair watched them drink from the bottles and were satisfied that it was just water. It was not uncommon to find people who took sips of alcoholic drink from paper-covered bottles in the park. However it was more unbecoming than illegal to drink alcoholic beverages in the parks and streets

"Sir, I have another question," said Ya. "Does our present day lifestyle and food habits the reason for us falling ill frequently? What is required for good health and happiness?"

"Modern lifestyle requires us to regulate our food-intake and add body exercises like Yoga Aasanas into our schedule before it is too late," said Movan. Ya nodded his head and said, "I agree."

Movan continued. "Affluence leads to excessive wastage of food on the table; Deliberate, forceful voluntary regulation can stop us from straining the nature. Food is first that we want again and again. Rest and sleep come next but only after food is eaten. Defense from injuries and illnesses is vital."

"What about it when we are old and weak?"

"Submitting to the caretaker for bath, toilet, food, etc., is required when we are old, weak, or sick. It is improper to fight the caretaker in disguised protest. The old and weak are happy if they get 24-hr electricity, water, food, shelter and essential materials. They would vote for a candidate whose party provides them."

Movan continued. "For me, food is selective. I cannot eat anything or everything. I am choosy. This is essential for my health and wellbeing. I eat good food. I got a clue why people cannot change their food habits. Parents especially mothers are responsible for our food habits learnt from infancy. I am not surprised if I can buy food rather than cook it myself at home but it's not the question of money; it is cleanliness and freshness. I can not imagine cattle as meat on the table. One who has no qualms about killing animals, would kill humans with no remorse of any kind.

"I fight those adverse conditions that affect my health. I provide my body and mind ammunition, viz. proper food, rest and exercise to win in life."

"What about Yoga Aasanas when we are old and weak?"

"Exercises are essential for the old but if the individual is weak then he or she has to recover from weakness to resume doing exercises.

"Society gives much respect to elderly people but dislike how some elders take undue advantage and force their outdated views on public affairs," said Movan.

"What about history?" asked Ya. Movan thought for a while and then said in a low voice, "History is what man writes from memory and observation but the future is what he shapes by utilizing his skills and knowledge."

Ya was silent for a minute. He liked what Movan said about history. A gentle breeze blew in his face and brought comfort to his dry skin.

Ya had come to the park straight from his office. He had traveled in a bus sitting on the window seat and the wind blowing in his face through the bus window from outside. It caused his skin to dry out giving him a dry feel.

He took out the bottle of water from his briefcase and the kerchief from his pant pocket. He poured some water on the kerchief. He wiped his face and felt the freshness that followed.

"How do we balance our acts between our own welfare and the welfare of the people around us, Sir?" Ya asked Movan.

" It is courage and boldness," said Movan. "It is with courage and fearlessness that we go along with our parents, teachers, relatives, neighbours, etc. for the welfare of all, even at our own cost."

"Where does human conscience come from? " asked Ya.

"We can only guess. My guess is that it comes from our parents and ancestors just as our body does. Our conscience is formed in the fertilized ovum, which as it grows learns to copy and tries to fit in with the surrounding human activities."

"Sir, you said you are guessing."

"Yes, Ya," said Movan. "I am only guessing. But modern science gives ample fodder to us to guess some of the explanations. For example I believe that our brain is the seat of mind. Our mind is the seat of our thought process and memory all of which together develop conscience that directs our actions, both good and bad. Our conscience is our property, which we develop as we grow. Our conscience guides us through our life. It makes up our life's directions, success, failure, retrials, lies and truths. I have learnt not only from books and from educational institutions but also from other sources. Good and sturdy conscience is my path to happiness, and it has been the ultimate teacher."

"Whom do you follow, Sir, in life?" asked Ya.

"Whom do I Follow? Simple," said Movan coolly. "I Follow not others but my conscience, my inner voice formed as I grew up, defining my conviction on all matters."

"Is your mind helping you?" asked Ya.

"My mind can make me happy, make me feel tense, feel afraid, become devotional, recall events I saw or I did before and build my personality. My mind can picturize a lot of scenes by imagination when I see through my eyes, read books, newspapers; watch TV etc. and hear through my ears. Feeling insecure is my inborn defensive character. Only my experience and MWC (Mind, Wisdom, Conscience combination) helps me overcome insecurity."

Movan looked at Ya. Ya was listening and preparing himself to ask the next question.

"Inborn defensive character. What is it?"

"When in danger we try to get away from the scene because of our inborn defensive character," replied Movan.

"I believe in discussion and hope to clear my doubts about so many things," said Ya changing the topic.

"What we believe need not be the truth," said Movan. "My hazy and uncertain thoughts that originate in my conscience become clearer, wiser, easier, and printable when I talk about them or begin to write them down. Imagination and prediction are my mental functions that arise out of my brain-embedded knowledge, info, beliefs, conscience and conviction."

"What is honesty, Sir?" asked Ya.

"Honesty is a long-term commitment. It could even be a life-long commitment and often causes temporary setback but only honesty keeps our conscience neat and spotless."

"I do not understand the meaning of the word honesty," said Ya. "Could you elaborate?"

"It is difficult to explain the meaning of honesty," said Movan calmly. "When I say I am doing my job honestly, it means I am doing my work to the best of my ability. I am sincere in carrying out the task given to me. But let me look into the dictionary."

Movan always carried a small dictionary in his bag. Whenever he had a difficult word he consulted the dictionary.

"The Oxford Dictionary gives the meaning of honesty as the quality of being honest," Movan was looking at the word 'honesty'. "Honest is truthful and sincere."

"Not concealing anything say from the employer or the boss. Right?" asked Ya.

"Yes," replied Movan. "We get paid for work and we are expected to be truthful and sincere at work, in which case the wages we get are fairly earned. An honest living is one in which the plumber or the electrician or even a doctor would charge a reasonable fee for work done."

"As an employee of the Government in a capitalist country a youth would gain stability and security of job. But honesty would not help much."

"When a person is a member of a team then that person has to follow the leader of the team. In the offices of a government department all the staff will work honestly if the supervisor is honest. A honest and sincere Prime Minister would ensure that his government is free from corruption and other ailments."

"A simple and straight-forward person is the best example of being honest," said Ya. "We serve honest food when we serve fresh clean food. When we do not short-change our customers then we are being honest."

"Why blame eager and ignorant patients who fall for the promises of dishonest quacks? Healthcare cost hit the roof and patient bit the floor. As if it is not enough to have developed deadly diseases, economically weaker patients embrace dishonest quacks thereby multiplying misery."

"It looks like only an honest student would learn the meaning of honesty," said Ya. "Some of the information I give honestly may be incomplete, inaccurate or false but I still record it for future generation to examine and verify."

"We got to express our thoughts and publish our views," said Movan reflecting upon what Ya said. "What we say will vanish but what we write down remains until the book stays on the bookshelf."

"There are so many aggressive young enthusiastic social workers that, if they preserve their honesty and integrity, will shine in due course."

"Never mind what others say so long as I have faith in the correctness of my work. Defeat comes because I dither and doubt my aim and reason."

"The most confusion I got into was when elders advised me that I have rights to work but not its rewards. I always eagerly awaited my payday. "

"Thank you, Sir," said Ya. "Let us meet again tomorrow evening. Good night, Sir." Ya picked up his briefcase and walked away. "Good night," said Movan and watched him hurrying down the path between rows of flowering plants. Ya reached the gate and went out of sight.

2

The gates of the park are opened for about 3 hours in the morning and about 5 hours in the evening. Usually the gates are closed for the night at about 9. Parks are meant for walks by citizens and not used as a place to eat lunch or as a resting place in the night.

Movan had his morning stroll as usual but he did not sit on the bench. He took a few rounds in the park and left to return home soon after. He expected Ya to appear in the evening when Movan can spend some time talking to him. Movan had no one to talk to. He had so many ideas and thoughts in his mind but everybody was busy with work. Talking to Movan only bored them. They did not find any substance in what Movan discussed

Movan eats his lunch at home around 1 in the afternoon. His wife Meenu cooks food for herself and also lets Movan sit down with her for lunch. Their house is the only structure on the site measuring 30 feet by 40 feet. There were similar houses on either side of Movan's, forming a row on the 25 feet wide black-topped street.

Movan and Meenu were the only residents in the big 2 BHK house. BHK stands for bedroom, hall and kitchen. Both of their children were grown-ups, married and lived in far away cities with their families.

Movan reads the newspaper after lunch reclining on the bed against raised pillows. He munches on peanuts and chews a couple of sweet candies until he reads sparsely 6 or 7 pages of the English language newspaper and before stretching himself flat on the bed. When his eyes become drowsy, he lowers the pillow and rests his head on just one 4-inch thick pillow. He falls asleep in about a minute.

The surroundings of the house has high decibel level of noise from early morning till late in the night. Movan packs his ears with rubber stoppers in order to keep away the loud noises from outside the house and from the nearby street. To be able to take a nap in the afternoon is one of life's pleasures Movan looks forward to after lunch. The rubber stoppers in Movan's ears keep noise away from disturbing his short slumber. His nap lasts for about one half to one hour. After getting up he goes to the toilet and smokes a cigarette. Then he prepares a cup of tea. Meenu meanwhile also takes a nap after lunch and rises a little later. Movan puts on his clothes and leaves for a walk.

Movan walked to the park which is about a kilometer from his home. Movan gets some exercise by this walk to and from the park regularly. There were a few other walkers in the park and Movan joined them in the walk. Soon he saw Ya approaching him.

"Hello, Sir," cried Ya. "Good evening."

"Good evening," replied Movan turning his head to see Ya's face. Ya appeared tired after work and after a long bus travel to the park. Ya lived with his parents in a house located on the same street as the one beside the park. The office where Ya worked closed at 4 in the afternoon and Ya could reach the park by 5 p.m., when the rays of the sun in the western sky were oblique. The shades of the trees and plants were stretched out under them. The gentle breeze blowing from the east swayed the shadows of the trees and plants from side to side.

"What is in your mind today, Sir?" asked Ya.

"It is about the need for assistants in getting work done in workshops and factories," replied Movan.

"Employers are wary of employing workers who hold degrees and diplomas if the latter consistently fail to do the given work as efficiently as expected."

"How best the employee can handle real issues in the work place is what tells us about the education and training the employee claims to own."

"It is possible to choose workers for ordinary jobs but for specialized jobs finding good and efficient workers is quite difficult."

"It takes at least a month for a new employee to settle down in his job. The employer has to be patient and let the new employee adjust to the new task. The work is not exactly the same as he did it in his college lab or at his previous employment."

"If the employee is hired for personal, communal or political reasons and not because of his qualifications then any employer, private or public would find such employee a big burden and liability."

"Some political leaders who become ministers or other office bearers in the government hire their party workers as a quid-pro-quo for winning in the elections. Such workers might take undue advantage of their positions in the government and do little or no work for the government. They would collect bribes for themselves or for their political bosses. Bribe taking is livelihood for a large proportion of people."

"Bribe-takers are angry at the new government and are looking for ways to teach a lesson to the latter by conspiracies not easily detected."

" Human nature is to get something in return for what we give. Men and women always do it but taking bribe for government work is corruption."

"The fact that the government person who accepts bribe does it under cover itself indicates that it is a stealthy operation and anti-social."

"What about female workers, Sir?" asked Ya.

"I do not know much about women other than my mother, sisters, wife, aunts, grandmother, teacher, workers all of whom are proud of me." Movan was thinking what to say about female workers. "I wonder if females are born physically weaker than males on purpose to fulfill any requirement in their natural functions."

"I am proud to be a father of a female child (now mother of her own daughter) and give credit to my wife for bearing and bringing her up."

"Breaking convention of including only males in line I have included all the females in our extended family tree in my book Adyar Gopal World."

"Employees are forced to retire at certain age but self-employed professionals can continue to work. I pursued my hobbies rather than work after retirement."

"Should salaries be taxed, Sir?"

"Tax is payable for a portion of total income calculated after deducting the exemption limit," explained Movan. "Every worker does not earn more than the amount exempted from income tax. For salary income beyond the tax exempted limit even the salaried class has to pay income tax."

"The employer is obliged to deduct tax before paying the salary," interjected Ya.

"Yes, Ya. The tax might be deducted at source (TDS) but the worker can calculate his income tax and get refund if the TDS is more than tax due. As a small time self-employed professional I kept my books of account myself to avoid falling into a trap and be accused of cheating on taxes. For a job educational and experience certificates are needed but for starting up our own business we need real know-how, a lot of money and motivation."

"Even if my intention was not to evade tax, the income tax department will consider me to have done an unlawful act if I do not file my tax return for my income beyond the exemption limit."

"Unexpected instant income puzzles my mind," said Ya. Ya was paid bonus of over ten thousand rupees for the year by his employer. "Lumpsum income ultimately makes me happy because I can now reset my priorities to a beneficial higher level. I am elated when I do any work that fulfils my aspirations even if my work isn't appreciated by my own relatives, friends or acquaintances."

"Increase in world population is big natural calamity for which Nature will devise unpredictable tool to restore normalcy, slowly but surely."

"Man's nature is the same whether he is white, black, brown or yellow, Chinese, Caucasian or Mixed, he laughs and cries, his doldrums similar."

"Our body is structured to withstand all kinds of assaults of nature but we are at least a decade behind in ability to face newer onslaughts."

"What is accident?" Ya asked.

"What is accident? Something go unexpectedly wrong. Not wrong for Nature. For nature there is no real accident. Everything is right for Nature. When something goes wrong it is for us the things go wrong. Not for Nature things go wrong. Accidents happen because of human incompetence. Wrong for humans but right for Nature. By simulating Nature we can avoid accidents."

"Moments of joy must outnumber moments of sorrow both of which result from my being alive and sensitive. Both brought on by Nature or myself."

"Whatever happens on this earth is limited on account of natural facility. Even our mind can not reach outside nature. Yet we attempt to go beyond nature and succeed in guessing."

"Much of what I do happens because of constitution of my body. Many bodily processes are involuntary. It is easier to go along with Nature."

"Most of the work I was ever engaged in was basic necessity for me to live and hence I was bound with Nature that lead me to do good things."

"There is no magic and no mantra of any kind in my growing up into a man. I could not by nature become a tree, a lake, or a pig if I wanted to."

"Civilization stands against Nature. Nature over time demolishes man's structures. Men rejuvenate and reconstruct civilization. This repeats."

"My mind as if trudges along poorly maintained shores of a rapid stream; remains alert to prevent a slip that will result in a fall and I drown."

"We often make wild guesses and go on to stress that what we say is true," said Ya. "To the listeners we say "I am convinced that this.. and that..." Our conviction is only judgmental belief rooted in our mind and we think it is true top to bottom."

Movan leaned back and rested his head on the top of back-rest of the cement bench. Ya looked at Movan and understood that the Senior was tired after the lengthy talk. There were more walkers in the park today and many of them were women in colourful sarees. The men wore pants and shirts.

After about 2-3 minutes, Movan took out the water bottle and poured some water into his open mouth and swallowed it little by little. He was wetting his mouth rather than quenching his thirst. Ya also drank some water from his water bottle and thus both got refreshed.

The discussion resumed.

"Whom do we pray if at all. Sir?" asked Ya.

"I fail to understand how even the most faithful would assume that any prayers would be answered positively if expensive gifts were offered? I have come to realize that unless I kneel down and beg for favours and gifts, I will be ignored; many entities will ignore a silent aspirant. Giving gifts is not an easy job because the gift given must not only be useful but also reveal the personalities of both giver and receiver. We give gifts to please the receiver."

"If the gift is left behind then we are puzzled. Aren't we?" asked Ya.

"In India it was assumed that by pouring ghee into the burning Yajna fire the ghee is transported to the gods," replied Movan. "It was theorized that any gift dropped in the Yajna fire would become ash and get transported to the entity the gift was meant to be given to. The receiver of the gift was an abstract and the giver was convinced of the truthfulness of the theory."

"There is a little selfishness in the act of giving gifts. We desire to live well. Our desire to live is strong but not strong enough to counter unscientific beliefs. We create a scene with fire of Yajna and burning of wood and ghee. We recite Manthras loudly and clearly. We sing in praise of the gods. The ceremony might impress upon those who believe in performing Yajna to satiate God."

Ya took out his mobile phone and switched it on to see what time it was. It was nearing 6.30 p.m. He looked at Movan. But Movan was not giving attention to Ya's moves. He went on with the discussion.

"My mind is my virtual expanse limited only by my knowledge and belief, the last keeps changing along with more of facts exposed and proved. I now do not look for direction in scriptures and religious books because what is given in them is mostly outdated and outmoded to be valid today and now."

"But prayer assumes the existence of the prayed," said Ya.

"Yes, it does," replied Movan. "My stomach does not permit me to sit in one place for hours together like they say for performing religious self-punishment or long prayers. As a human being I am challenged by everything; the sky, wind, earth, water, fire, other human beings, animals, etc., but I keep winning."

"Common Law follows human conscience and affirms good habits," said Ya. "Booked Law will adhere to man and society provided it reflects the Common Law. It is our choice to follow the Common Law but it is our duty to follow booked law of the country we live in."

It was now time to leave. Both Movan and Ya got up and Movan led the path towards the park gate.

"Good night, Ya."

"Good night, Sir."

3.

The skies were overcast but Movan thought the weather will be pleasant once the rains came and went. He carried the umbrella if in case he was in the street when it rained. When Movan reached the park the bench was dry. A short while later it began to rain in tiny drops. Movan did not open his umbrella. He liked the rain drops touching his hair and descending in to his scalp. He liked the drops that fell on his cheeks and open arms. But the rain was swept away by the wind that followed. And soon Ya was standing in front of Movan.

"Sit down, Ya," said Movan. Ya did not carry umbrella with him. He was pretty sure the rain will be of a short duration if at all. He sat down on the bench about an arm's distance from Movan.

"I was thinking," began Movan. "A Structure of Education that will create a workforce of skilled men and women ready to work in farms, industries and professions is needed.

"No matter what happened in the past, even in the remotest, my present and future are shaped by what I think is best in the circumstances."

"I think, not only India but also every other country on earth is progressing due to benevolent Modern Science. Plan to live good long life!"

"Young men and women must develop boldness to become rich, famous, marry very beautiful person, build palatial house, etc., as early as possible in their life."

"There is no shortage of advisers; information may be incomplete, stale, out of place, impractical, lacks incentive, purpose and worthy goal."

"About 33% of us will be dead when India that is contemplated now takes shape in 2030; those alive then would say 'this is not good enough.'"

"Our ancient culture (Sanskrit Language, Religious practices, etc.), which our women deeply honour, has kept India united in its diversity."

"The fact that more than 120,00,00,000 people enjoy freedom, etc., in India as a nation is itself a great triumph. Bharath is here to stay."

"What is true today may not have been true yesterday and may not be true tomorrow. Truth is relative. Deviations in truth are hard to notice."

"I make the most of what I have today such as my home, education, neighbourhood, and not harp on what I had in my past. I look to the future."

"But Sir," interjected Ya. "You started to say something about the structure of education in India."

"Yes. I am coming to that," replied Movan. "You see the Indian Structure of Education I hope changes into a focused and purposeful machination in which a career for 14 yr old 8th pass is built-in."

"I want to see a new structure of education in India. The British established a Structure of Education in India with 11th class as School Leaving (SL) class. I think 8th is better for India of the present. The present Structure of Education with 10th class as the School Leaving (SL) is unsuitable for India of 2016. Make 8th pass as the SL."

"People talk about schooling and learning being different and about need of a paradigm shift in our education system but not about how to do it."

"The government may make 8th class pass as the School Leaving (SL) and diversify 9th onward for various careers including Medicine and Engineering."

"Making 8th pass as the School Leaving class followed by career-specific diverse classes would be a paradigm shift in our education system."

"Those 14 yr old 8th pass youngsters who chose higher education are admitted into the courses meant for them in new Structure of Education."

"When I had reached the 8th class, I was 14 years and receptive to career guidance like all youngsters of that age, from parents and others. I, like everyone else, was not aware how important it was to begin early my pursuit of a career, supported by my parents and teachers alike. With only one or two children, the parents can focus better on their child's career, starting at age 14 and select one that's most suitable."

"At the age of 14 a child is anxious to achieve and wishes to prepare himself for his future mainly by looking for support from his father."

"System of Education available in the region determines the career chosen by the child, the father or the mother and not merely the ambition."

"The government decides the kind of system of education for schools, which prepare the child in taking up a career most suitable for him/her."

"Ordinary people normally would send their children to local schools that adopt the government system of education and are easily accessible."

"There are many careers such as priests and other religious offices for which the regular schools do not provide path, education or training."

"Indian Constitution gives freedom of religion; does not promote any particular religion and therefore religions are not part of curriculum."

"'Morals' was a subject included in the school curriculum but religion was never made a subject to be taught and examinations conducted in."

"Language(s), arithmetic, basic science and basic social studies are the main subjects that are included in the curriculum in all schools."

"An appropriate career is chosen for their child by the parents by applying their knowledge and belief so that the same will bring happiness."

"Before a career is chosen for the 14-year old child, the parents would make sure that the required education and training are within reach."

"Since early 20th Century Indian education especially the Secondary School Pre-matric syllabus has been oriented towards degree certificate."

"For many careers such as a potter, SSLC or the degree are unnecessary and the years spent in the school after 8th class is a waste of time."

"If a 14-year old is not told to focus on a certain career and set on its path for education and training then the child will drift aimless."

"A career chosen by a 14-yr old child can be modified and changed later according to circumstances and capacity and accessibility of chances."

"Making a 14-yr old child go through and study for many years after his 8th class without a definite career in sight is an unhelpful outcome."

"All kinds of occupations could become welcome careers and provide us financial security and happiness in life if planned and pursued early in life."

"Earlier we decide on our life's career better could we decide our place of residence and style of living thus gaining control and security."

"The main purpose of deciding on a career early is to get the child think about his future independence and looming responsibilities in life."

"The 8th pass being sufficient for most of the skills and occupations, the diversification process of education and training may begin with the 9th class."

"Management of the adolescent by the parents is as tricky as of toddler but the situation differs owing to change in child's way of thinking."

"To keep 14-yr old away from vices and bad company it is useful to firmly advise him to take up education and training for his future career early in life."

"A 14-yr old is at the right age for making him love and respect his country, culture and tradition and allowed in nationalistic activities."

"There is a high point in life of a child after 8th class when he/she and parents decide if they select self-employment as the career or not."

"A 14-yr old girl would be wise to listen to her mother and other older women regarding her future career, as she would herself be a mother."

"Wise parents make a list of careers for their 14-yr old to select from. The child then would work harder and with determination towards it."

"Parents are directly responsible till 14 but later it is the school, friends and the government that intervene to influence the child's ID."

"Govt's influence is uppermost since examinations are conducted and degree necessary for child to take up career is issued by Government agencies."

"Diversification of courses starts from 12th class onwards at present, forcing students to delay choosing of their career by 4 years in a virtual maze."

"Since about a hundred years, the Indian 14-yr old child has been forced to wait for another 4 years to begin career education and training."

"Parents, especially the mother, would want her 14-yr old child to live a happy life for which he/she selects a family oriented occupation."

"It takes time to change the norm but an 8th pass 14-yr old may be permitted to join ITI-like training institutes to begin his quest for a career."

"Smart parents treat their 8th pass 14-yr old with love and respect because he or she is going to be the future torchbearer of the family."

"Smart parents put their 8th pass 14-yr old on a track to spend the next 4 years in building the blocks for a career education and training."

"Even MBBS or BE could be the career options for an 8th pass 14-yr old and the focus would provide the child an aim to cling on and get busy."

"Let 8th pass be the new school graduation from where the young one will embark on a planned, parent-approved and self-chosen career option."

"14 years of life, love and activity since birth forms a big chunk of lifespan and passing 8th class is an achievement equal to a medal of merit."

"Up to 8th Class be common for all careers and 8th Pass the standard Graduation following which be Specialization towards the chosen career."

"At present even 20 years study in schools and colleges usually does not make us READY TO START WORKING in farms, industries and professions."

"At present a student after 8th Class crams lessons to pass the exams, the subjects of which may not be applicable to her/his career chosen."

"Our lives' most crucial years, in which we prepare ourselves for a bright future career, are 15th to 20th, which need guidance from parents."

"Our life's 15th and 16th years are for honing skills and 17th to 20th are for specializing in various professions, so help us, Educators!"

"Education is predominantly a state subject and therefore it is left to each state to declare 8th class as standard educational qualification."

"If we start at 14th yr by first listening to our parents and friends and then deciding on our own, we can choose the career and excel too."

"Declaring 8th class pass as School Leaving (SSLC) or Matric class, and 10th, 12th and degree as post Matric the government would redirect education."

"Youth are becoming literate very much sooner than yesterday and making them wait till 16th year for Matric Certificate is out of place and cruel."

"What is learnt during eight years from 1st to 8th class in these costly days should be highly valued and honoured making 8th Pass as Matric."

"At present the 8th Pass 14 yr., old youth is groping in the dark as regards the future since she/he is not shown light to get out of the school tunnel."

"At present S. S. L. C. (Matric) is upon completion of 10th Class, out of which 9th and 10th could be replaced with career relevant subjects."

"The government must make it easy for the 8th Pass 14 yr old youth to take up the line of education and training that fits her/his career."

"At present the classes 9th and 10th are trackless and 11th and 12th are excluding common career pursuits like farming and self-employment."

"Prospects of a good marriage depend not so much on the degree held as on the chosen career, profession and employability of the groom/bride."

"After 8th class and 14 years of age it is important from where we get the facts, skills and wisdom. We get them from our parents, friends, books and the Internet."

"The age of 14 years is a point where every youth has an opportunity to mend and bend and fall back on the track with self-will and self-power."

"The will and vigour at the age of 14 needs grooming and goading to kindle its fire and exploit its force and not shut up in weird syllabi."

"What should the government do, Sir?" asked Ya giving a hint to Movan that it is about time to go home.

"Government's first step to restructure education: Declare 8th pass as School Leaving (Matric) level and as First Graduation (Not Drop-outs)."

"In the new structure of education the study of Agriculture, Animal husbandry, Textiles, Commerce, Languages, Humanities, Arts and Crafts, Basic Sciences, etc., is taken up 9th onwards."

"That I think is fair enough, "said Ya. "But will the government listen?"

Both Movan and Ya got up and Movan led the path towards the park gate. "Good night, Ya."

"Good night, Sir."

4.

Ya was already sitting on the bench when Movan arrived for his evening walk today. "Hello, Sir," said Ya greeting Movan. "Hello," said Movan. Movan respected Ya's wish to clear the doubts regarding various points of interest. It was not a tutorial or a teaching session but only a one-to-one discussion between an elderly man and a young man.

"How are you today?" asked Movan as he dusted the seat with his towel and made himself comfortable.

"I am fine, Sir," replied Ya. "Let us continue with our discussion of the structure of education in India. You said that in the structure of education, the 8th is School-Leaving Class /Matric. From 9th onwards the students choose one among the six Career Courses from basic Science to Professional."

"Yes. If youth is not engaged with a career by the age of 14 years then the youth will drift into unpredictable adventurism like an untamed horse."

"Lucky are the parents who agree among themselves and make up their mind as to what career their child who is turning 14 should follow up."

"In making up mind as to the career for her child turning 14, the mother often can not think right, being overprotective and extra-cautious."

"Economy of any country depends upon the opportunities its population finds to harness the available resources for use on a permanent basis."

"Parents are at a loss to know what to do if an 8th pass 14 yr old child not study well in the 9th class. Allow them to take up a safe job."

"By refusing to allow 8th Pass 14 yr., old take up a safe job, India is denying itself a large human force from contributing to its G. D. P."

"We fell into the trap well laid by competitors abroad that raised the bogey of child labour when they found our products were nosing them."

"The Government and the wise people must direct the youngsters by suitable Structure of Education towards goals that bring prosperity to all."

"The present system of 10th class as Matriculation or School Leaving class doesn't allow for diversification earlier and creates 'drop-outs'. By terming youngsters who left school before 10th class as 'drop-outs' we are making it all worse for them and pushing them down further. Media can in due course turn the tables for the better or for the worse just as they termed the 8th class pass leaving school as a 'dropout.'"

"Grading our curriculum in such a way that schooling is unbroken till 10th class while 8th is more convenient hampers freedom of choice."

"The present Structure of Education forces children into the 9th to 12th classes wherein a large number of students can not get through."

"New Structure of Education doesn't mean stop after 8th class. Everyone continues classes that are meant to prepare her/him for a career."

"Make 8th class pass the major stepping-stone by introducing a New Structure of Education, after which students take up study in courses that they fit in."

"A Certificate of completion of a course by post-8th class students will enable employers to hire them as trainees/apprentices for 1-2 years."

"If the government declares passing 8th class as the end of schooling then millions of youngsters will begin training for the career of their choice."

"The New Structure of Education you are proposing," said Ya, "would eliminate 9th to 12th classes from most of the career courses by making 8th class the end of schooling. Doesn't it?"

"It does," replied Movan coolly. "In fact a majority of careers chosen by youngsters do not need subjects taught in present 9th to 12th classes, which only dislodge their ambitions. When the youngster knows that subjects he is studying in the 9th to 12th classes are not going to be of any help to him he gets frustrated. He considers that he is being forced to learn what he has no interest in."

"Make 8th pass the end of schooling and 9th the beginning of learning as to how to live with an occupation the student and his parents wish to take-up."

"The class 9th to 12th is a long journey and about half of the students do not benefit from what they learn in them being inapt career wise."

"What is inapt for most of the careers such as the syllabus in the 9th to 12th class may be avoided if we adopt a new Structure of Education."

"I appeal to the wise men in our government to change our Education system to make the most of our young receptive bright minds of students especially in their 15th to 18th years of life."

"At present there is no choice but to continue schooling until 12th class, which be set right by making the 8th pass as School Leaving class."

"A career in agriculture begins at 15th year provided our Structure of Education is reformed and 8th pass declared as School Leaving class."

"A career in carpentry, plumbing, painting, masonry, garment making, are all staple careers needing two years apprenticeship after 8th class. "

"Convert 9th class into post-Matriculation class (as against 11th as at present) and reap focused learning by well-guided lively youngsters."

"Naming 8th class pass as the School Leaving class is a major shift in education system and it will not happen without government initiative."

"Although naming 8th class pass as School Leaving class is a big decision, it only builds an earlier platform to embark upon careers sooner."

"Although naming 8th class pass as School Leaving class is big decision, doing so does not alter basic pattern of imparting skills to youth."

"Change Structure of Education. Abolish the present 9th to 12th run-of-the-mill, go-nowhere classes replacing them with career aimed options."

"Not all parents are rich enough to give education to their children their way; poor and middle class parents take what the government gives."

"Even after 12 years of learning as at present a student is not ready for a job because she has not been given education to acquire a skill."

"I pity those students who slog in the schools from 9th to 12th classes, by-heart set answers to questions, pass the exams but have no skills."

"Present 9th to 12th classes impart education to become a clerk, a teacher in lower school or study further but not go for other occupations."

"Avoid shaming 8th pass students who leave school to take up occupations as school dropouts. Make 8th class pass a graduation in education."

A child gets education and passes the 8th class examinations; then child is ready for better education than the present 9th to 12th classes.

"What a child learns in 9th to 12th classes at present makes him a scholar but unfit for job until he takes another four years of education."

What we learn in 9th to 12 classes is hard to unlearn; therefore to learn a trade or profession begin after 8th pass, so help us, Government."

"We are inviting heavy responsibility by making India a developed country; no worry if 8th class continues as a pressure point for the poor."

"I will talk to people who have the authority to change the education system whenever I get a chance," said Ya. "This is really a revolutionary approach to reform education in India."

Movan had spoken in such a lucid manner that Ya thought that Movan had already formed his opinion long back and it was an easy game for him to put forth his ideas in one go.

"When passing 8th class becomes an important event in our Structure of Education then students join 9th that caters to their chosen careers."

"Spare the rod but don't spoil the child is the modern saying; spare the child from burden of subjects not connected to the selected career. 9th –12th classes at present discourage those who want to earn by 17th year. Use these years instead to exact career education and training."

"Watch how fast GDP will increase if and when 8th class pass is made School Leaving class. Government should modify grading education levels. A good primary school is the one in which teachers keep an eye on pupils to prevent them from drifting away from studies and good manners."

"The good school makes up for any deficiency at home and often helps parents learn from their wards ways to improve their manners and methods. Delaying vocational education until completion of 12th class is unsuitable for people who must earn their livelihood by 17th year of life."

"Most vital is the age of a person, and once past a certain age activities get restricted. Agility at 15, at 21and at 31 is not the same. Boys and girls at 15 become most eager to help themselves and everyone around them including their country provided they are guided well."

"We abuse those enterprising poor youngsters who took 8th class pass as enough for the time to embark on a career by calling them 'dropouts'. The term 'school dropout' indicates the student to have stopped studying. If an 8th class pass opts for a career he is not a school dropout. Not all students have resources to join medical, dental, engineering and similar educational colleges. They look for other affordable ways. Only the governments can make changes to the Structure of Education these days; such as making 8th class pass as the School Leaving class."

"School Leaving doesn't mean curbing studies. It's only a landing. Presently it is the 10th, from where students launch the career course of choice. If there are only Non-stop buses then we cannot alight at a place of our choice, like the present Non-stop education past 8 till 10th class."

"Years and semesters are natural but Non-stop education till 10th is irrational. Let them alight gracefully after 8th pass with graduation. After 8th class pass let there be 1st and 2nd PVC (Pre-Vocation Course) and not 9th and 10th class. 11th and 12th will be Training classes."

"A student likes to do service to humanity but he/she needs guidance; he/she will imbibe best at age of 15 years of age, i.e. at 8th class pass. A child gets prodded to emulate great persons of the past but he/she is miseducated and misguided and waste talent in 9th to 12th classes."

"Aim is to teach children that come from different financial backgrounds how to earn their livelihood; not to make them saints or saadhus. Students do not consider advice as pressure such as from parents, teachers and friends. Parents advice their wards out of their experience. Responsibility of parents for their wards is most significant because they have to nurture the children to shape the future of the Nation. Where there is will there are ways. Will Indian wise men coax the governments to make it easy for youngsters to get education and a career?"

"The bond of parents with their children is to be strengthened and not weakened by outside stories and statistics of pressure and prejudice. Keeping children engaged in reading, doing odd jobs at home, serving at prayer halls, etc., by parents will keep them safe from bad company."

"'Freedom' and 'Liberty' refer to rights of the citizens to walk along the path laid down by Law and not to disrupt Order by misbehaviour. Spoken law comes from Court Judges and written law comes from Legislature; only these power bodies can reform our Structure of Education."

"All professional colleges and vocational institutions will in due course admit 8th class pass students to introduce them into their courses. Catching them young helps in two ways. One they get to aim for a career of their choice early and two, they steer clear of being jobless."

"Children of working mothers learn life's contemporary ways thoroughly when trained and mature caretakers attend to them in daycare centers. Governments could help parents by recognizing 8th class pass as end of first phase of schooling and beginning of training for many careers."

"Now let me say something about tobacco," said Movan, wanting to discuss another of his pet subjects.

"No problem, I am game," said Ya calmly. Tobacco was a subject which had been extensively discussed in news channels and newspapers.

"One of the causes of increase in usage of harmful drugs by youngsters is the campaign against smoking from every quarter including the Law."

"Anti-smoking lobby will not get any donations from the cigarette manufacturers if the latter suffer loss because of activity of the former."

"If tea and coffee are foods then tobacco and alcohol are also foods. Moderation in consumption will keep away man from other harmful drugs."

"If a few articles by eminent scientists raising doubt in cause-effect link of cancer with tobacco appear in newspapers then the deal is off."

"Tobacco farming is wide-spread and a large population depend on it for their livelihood. Alternative crops have to be initiated to stop tobacco farming."

"I was like any other adolescent, later a young man was a prey to vices but I found smoking cigarettes or chewing paan are the least harmful of vices."

"If there was ban on smoking in 1950-60s, like it is now, then I might have taken up some other vice such as drugs, alcohol, etc., as is happening now."

"I found drinking 4 cups of coffee or tea with/without sugar is worse for health than smoking ten cigarettes a day but all of them help man. Smokers are peace loving and not troublemakers and designating smoking areas in cities, airports, bus and railway stations makes us all a happy lot."

"Rise in use of drugs and alcohol is a counter-product of ban on smoking as the drudgery and boredom of 8-hr work needs recreation for youth. I believe that smoking cigarettes or bidi is the least harmful of recreations available to them."

"For me, smoking a cigarette (a habit not an addiction) helps in dieting, in moving bowels well, in refreshment and relaxing in-between work."

"Experimental animals are made to smoke more than 40 cigarettes a day to detect effects, is it not? Smoking like many things is double edged."

"A danger of smoking is fire coming off an unextinguished butt or a lighter, match box, etc. Another is chronic effect on respiratory tract."

"60 years from now there won't be any tobacco product available in the market. Man won't stop looking for other means, like liquor and drugs."

"At present there are millions of helpless innocent smokers on earth; the anti-tobacco lobby is shaming them. Governments are buckling under to the lobby."

"We got to live through many curses on the society one of them being the anti-tobacco curse. A day will come too late if at all to reinstate smoking as safe."

"Blowing out of proportion the cancers caused by tobacco, anti-tobacco activists have made life miserable for millions of smokers world over."

"Fire hazard is more likely than cancer by lighting up cigarettes and peril of dirt more likely than cancer by chewing tobacco; so take care."

Movan stopped talking and looked around. He had seen people smoking cigarettes in the park in the past but now there were none that dared to pull out a cigarette from the cigarette case that they might be carrying. Smokers who dared to smoke in the park were fined heavily. The Goods and Services Tax (GST) was 28% on cigarettes. Yet those who smoked were unable to quit the habit unless they took up drinking liquor or swallowing narcotic pills, stimulants, opiates such as Ganja or heroin, Marijuana, and tranquilizers, which ever suited their liking.

"Is GST on cigarettes only 28%?" asked Ya.

"I am not sure," replied Movan. "It could be more. Sipping tea, coffee, smoking cigarette, playing cards, chess, etc., is harmful in one or other way but not as much as drinking liquor daily."

"It is incredible that a cigarette smoker has to work against the government and a whole lot of non-governmental organizations to just enjoy a smoke."

Ya looked at the time on his mobile phone. Movan had a wrist-watch on his left wrist. The time was 6.40 and Ya thought it was time to wind up today's session. He stood up and looked at Movan's face. Movan looked at Ya and said, "Okay. I am ready. I go home and enter the bathroom. I sit on the toilet seat and smoke a cigarette. Smoking cigarette is probably the ultimate delight in my life at present. I am not ashamed to change my colours if it helps me to stop brooding over gory past inimical to my present affluence and future prospects. Good night, Ya."

"Good night, Sir."

5.

"Mothers are images of success," said Ya, after he took his seat beside Movan in the park. "A woman is not a success unless she gives birth and brings up a baby."

"My mother just like all mothers," rejoined Movan in the discussion immediately. "Could not shirk her responsibility towards her children, which is basic to continuation of life on earth."

"Right from the time of birth I wanted to draw the attention of people and things around me beginning from my mother, to fight through life."

"My motivation to live has been a woman all my life, be it the mother, sisters, wife, daughter or grand daughter in spite of any impertinence."

"I was made to learn so many things in which I was not interested during childhood and even later. My tries at self-education expanded my wisdom."

"Power of a woman is hidden behind her engaging appearance but it increases with her age and ultimately makes her use it to benefit society."

"Laws on human rights intrigue me. When an embryo, which the ignorant woman never wanted, is conceived then the Laws disregard human rights."

"I sympathize with judges when they decide if the human rights of the woman with unwanted embryo is more important or a living mass of cells."

"When I am aware that a National interest prevails over the personal benefit of a citizen then I understand why we need to save a girl child."

"It takes 9 months for a conception to result in birth. Citizenship claimed of the country of conception should be as valid as that of birth."

"Ya, what I am saying is private but the public is not interested. No one can settle matters in domestic quarrels. Being a husband and a provider I am all powerful but in front of my wife should I become just plain dust the way she decimates me? I am frugal and my wife I believe is stingy. We live together and therefore there is conflict regarding my spending habits."

"I am more liberal in the sense that I do not dictate terms to my wife or for that matter to any man or any woman."

"When a good-looking boy from a rich and powerful family offers to marry a girl he meets, the latter usually accepts his offer. Parents are wise if they do not object their wards from getting married to a counterpart of their well thought-out choice."

""For a parent the prospects of a good marriage for their ward may be important but it is the career that provides stability to wedded life."

"An educated woman takes up a job and likes to keep that job even after she gets married. There is conflict if the husband works in another city. Children are fed, educated, got a job/business, got married and moved, then the parents are left with surplus to fight among themselves."

"The Constitution is the guide for governance and to guide constitutional bodies and not, I believe, for forcing individuals in conduct of their private lives."

"In the Constitution, Equality is not based on birth, titles, etc. Even descendants of past rulers enjoy only the benefits of own labour."

"Living as a human being, as a citizen of a democratic country, a country with a liberal constitution is like living in heaven that we crave for."

"I fool myself if I try to treat everyone as equal. I feel at home with people of my race, religion, language etc., by my tribal instinct."

"Once I study and learn and start a project then I must educate others for support without which I won't succeed even if I am all-powerful."

"Getting out of the way of those who dislike our style will not help, especially in the case of our near and dear ones. They need our help."

"Sir, I think our life moves along because of the sun," said Ya trying to interject his thoughts in the discussion.

"The sun is responsible," replied Movan. "Yes, the red hot sun that is responsible for our daily routine and not the cock that crows and wakes us up at dawn."

"Sun helps me manage my days; the clock is a great gadget; keeps my moments on track. I learnt since long how to make the most of my leisure."

"It was water, sunlight and earth that brought about life on earth, the last of oxygen and glucose first. No water? Never will such a situation come about, hopefully."

"Time is out of control which fact I learnt before it was too late. For me to act next, my time arriving is as slow as 60 seconds/minute. The time gone went fast. The time arriving is slower by our imagination."

"I always have difficulty to comprehend time. Yesterday appeared to have passed at a high speed but now the next hour seems to be crawling."

"Time heals everything; especially the grief of loss of a dear one. Crying to heart's content till I overcome the grief is a personal remedy."

"Unsolvable problems raise their head from many quarters. Personal problems may be of body or of mind. I give them time to let go themselves."

"Do the positions of the stars and planets at the time of our birth determine our personality, life's successes and failures? No, they don't."

"I have learnt how to act deaf when I hear adverse comments from people around me so that both I and the other party have time to cool down."

"I have learnt that all preventive measures are important but most of the time my preventive measures are not enough for me to win."

"My destiny depends on the speed with which I grab opportunity to perform rather than how deeply I analyse its consequences. I often take risk."

"Our location is the center of our life for the moment. All we do from here is relative to date and time we do them. We record it for posterity's sake."

"I am rich and powerful because the society let me be. After I looked after myself now it is time to help my family, relatives, friends, etc."

"The world is factual multiplicity while my mind is a screen in which thoughts appear one at a time. My prowess to visualize world is tested."

"Other people might fail me but me is determined to look other ways where there is brightness and welcome sign to try again and succeed."

"Wow! This thought of yours is really great, Sir!" said Ya appreciating the mind-power of Movan, who had now practically become his mentor.

"Thanks," said Movan, and continued. "There is guideline for each and everything I do under instructions from others. For personal work I prepare my own guideline to succeed. When I complete a project successfully then I am ecstatic regardless of financial fruits, name and fame, rewards, accolades, and thumb downs."

"What about vested interests, Sir?" asked Ya. "The media have denigrated vested interest so much that it is now considered to be a path to corruption."

"Yes, it is a sorry state of affairs," replied Movan. ""Vested Interest" made me work hard for the good of my family, friends, region, language, community and Nation. Selfishness is the need of time. I was told repeatedly loudly that "vested interest" is a no-no for social causes. It turned out to be a trick to discourage private welfare schemes."

"When someone wants to make public his or her word or voice, apart from the press conference, the social media and mobilecast come abreast. We can publicize lies also through the media."

"Is it possible for any public person to switch the media (journalists) on or off at will? Some such persons have been successful, it seems."

"The media, all kinds of them, can make the voice of one into a roar of a million, if there is sense, substance and utility in it (the voice). The power of Media, all kinds, is like power of God. Man is the father of God and also of Media. When man needs help he recalls either One."

"Most of what I post in the social media impacts a small section of people, a section much larger than I am. I am a sand particle on the beach. But some news-feeds have a vast network to spread their lies (or truth, if they please). However, social media help people like me to express views in a civilized manner and thereby quench awful thirst for exhibition."

"I have a limited agenda but the tools like the social media are very vast and depending on the number of followers my spread is also limited."

"History keeps repeating and has neither beginning nor end. Ancient Indians avoided recording dates to refrain from writing personal taints."

"Give less importance to History in school syllabus so that what is written from memory and observation does not vitiate future prospects."

"We spend our precious first few years of life at home and in school and wish our parents and society take care so that we don't dropout by our weakness."

"Our educational qualification decide whom we work for. Parents and government help us acquire our intended education early to embark on a career."

"Self-employment is preferable," said Ya. "Great enthusiasm to start a business blinds us of the enormous responsibilities that hide behind it and need to be addressed simultaneously."

"That is correct," explained Movan. "Rules and regulations imposed by the government on hiring and firing by a business are usually hidden behind incentives offered to starters."

"Whose money is it anyway! Go for a government job if you want God's money to repay in next birth rather than work hard at your own business."

"After school and college I embarked as a self-employed professional; studied all Laws and Acts applicable so that I am not caught unawares."

"What I am telling you now is what I wish to put out for people to think over. Doing so helps me to kick-start my thinking whether it's right or not."

"I find that we choose our likes and dislikes on the basis of our customs, language, religion, castes, place of birth and place of residence."

"When I start a project, which depends on the performance of others, I shall not expect everyone to be as enthusiastic and efficient as I am."

"I am aware that my name, my parentage and my family oblige me to preserve our social value and respect so that members of my community feel proud to belong to our group. So are all decent people."

"I might be rich and powerful but when I help others with money and material I will be careful not to humiliate them for being in distress."

"When I want to giveaway (because I am rich and elderly) then, I feel, my wife and children are not eligible to receive my giveaways. They should stand in the wings."

"I face conflict of interest when some one close to me speaks against me and objects to what I truly believe in with full faith and in its aptness."

"I am free to do what I want in private but that is where I overlook the fact that I am watching myself if what I am doing is right or wrong."

"If I shut all communication lines and deal only with those activities of immediate concern then it's like fasting and can't last very long."

"I always look at the prospects. Is my decision hurting a few but bringing justice to the public in general and to my country in particular?"

"I cannot be a Russian, nor an American, nor a Chinese, a Japanese or any other National. I can only be an Indian and I feel proud to be one."

Ya became serious hearing this. He asked, "are you a politician, Sir?"

"No I am not a politician," replied Movan. "I am sure that Politics was not my cup of tea because I had wife and children to look after. Politicians can succeed well without a family."

"I am not a politician, only politically minded and so I do contribute my mite in nation building. For example, I support the recent Land Bill, which restores rights of the buyer of houses."

"I like to speak about various subjects but I also like to listen to different views on political, social, religious and other matters also."

"I can't forget the fact that my citizenship binds me with the country. I must fortify the bonds, not allow myself to be made a double agent."

Ya became careful now. He did not wish to provoke Movan to speak a lot about politics. He wished to change the subject.

"What are your interests and hobbies, Sir?"

"I saw a 1960s-movie made by a famous director recently," replied Movan. "Movies, books, crafts and everything created in India could be outstanding products."

"I am becoming more and more familiar with connecting to Internet using the broadband line and not spend hours trying to connect like before."

"In the Digital world, the Non-Netizens that is the computer illiterates will loose their ground even if they are otherwise well-educated."

"I know you are an author," said Ya. "And that you have written and published books in Hindi, English, Kannada and Konkani languages."

"Yes," replied Movan. "I won't know if my colleague, friend, relative, comrade, neighbour, etc., get offended when I write or say something that I know is a fact."

"Time, Surroundings, Social features, etc., keep changing. So, I stop reminding myself of any wrong-doings of anybody to keep myself from hating them."

"My face is a tool to show friendliness or enmity by smiling or grimacing but often I put on an appearance to suit the occasion and people."

"Peace of mind is not meant for the young. In my youth I was constantly agitated to acquire knowledge, skills, popularity and stood in front to observe and learn."

"I would not succeed in building up an amicable atmosphere with my neighbour if the latter is by all principles against my very existence there."

"I have learnt not to dislike a person or group that belongs to me and my country even if they often disagree with my actions and motives."

"The world as we see it today is the result of the toil of millions of humans; for some it is most livable, pleasant and for some it is bad."

"When we fall sick we become helpless," said Ya. "We got to go to a doctor. Don't we?"

"Yes, we need quick relief," replied Movan. Now there is a choice between Indian Medicine and Modern Medicine."

"There is need for more astute integration of Modern Medicine into Indian Medicine (mainly Ayurveda) to avoid layman's confusion at choice."

"These days one man cannot make basic changes in teaching Medicine such as merging Modern Medicine and Indian Medicine; we need a Committee of experts to do it."

"Indian Medicine has been kept aloof and unreformed. Its educators need to give up invalid theories and modernize more fully than at present."

"The Ayush (A.veda, Yoga, Unani, Siddha, H-pathy,) educators have to become bold like the household remedy users who discarded old theories."

"Patients especially in rural India cannot make informed decision if Ayush doctors claim cure for all diseases not disclosing the prognosis."

"Claiming divine attributes to medical theories we fool ourselves into stagnation, lack of innovation and forgo benefits of modern thoughts."

"We need to disconnect medical treatment from ghosts, spirits and from heavenly bodies because Medicine is plainly earth-bound common-sense."

"By relegating success in treating diseases to pleasure of heavenly bodies and not to proficiency of doctors we deflect from Modern Medicine."

"Modern Medicine is not just Allopathic. Modern Medicine has imbibed all kinds of medical systems including Ayurvedic, our own Indian system."

"Cannot marry a cock with a monkey. Ayurveda system has to change its basics to really become Indian Modern Medicine; not just 'Integrated'."

"Object is universal: human body and its health. Medical systems are different. One known to be most useful must become government-promoted."

"Treating diseases is not tailor-made since each individual is different in body, mind and intelligence. Prescriptions are written specifically."

"I guess 2 to 10 percent of our ailments are hereditary, so also ability of our body to overcome diseases. Information about health is vital."

"Cost of medical care is such that only rich people can afford the best modern medical treatment. Hard to say what is best going by results."

"Human endeavor in medical research slowed down turnover of world population over past sixty years. People live a longer and healthier life."

"Ailments and diseases treated and health restored by right kind of medical intervention but disinformation can make us pick the wrong kind."

"Love for Indian and the Ancient might be patriotism but when we need to pick a medical system for our well being we choose Modern Medicine."

"Small roadside shop-like clinics of licensed doctors are the best way to cater to healthy towns and cities. Pl modify licensing eligibility."

"Speculative statements from any source either ancient or popular and refuted by modern findings may be dumped for advancement in Medicine."

"Wise elderly people advise youngsters to get necessary experience of visiting a doctor before one gets really sick. Prevention is the best."

"Too many guidelines spoil the initiative and blunt the innovative but leaving everything to the doctor is unfit for health care of masses."

"Life as an economically weak person is not so bad as being advised to undergo costly treatment available for diseases with poor prognosis."

"When we do not have money to undergo costly treatment of diseases of poor prognosis then we better not make close relatives bear the burden."

"When we have a child who needs our savings for its future and we fall ill with a deadly disease of poor prognosis then our dilemma is cruel."

"It will be a tragedy for a parent and children alike when the former falls ill with a deadly disease of poor prognosis and costly treatment."

"Managing healthcare of the masses is different from treating individual cases. Even managing hospital is left to non-doctor administrators."

"Hospital doctors are immensely better equipped with all kinds of drugs and modern medical gadgets than individual practitioners in clinics."

"Only when we fall sick and our home remedies do not work within a short time then we visit a doctor and find how our doctor treats illnesses."

"I will not look for the needle in a straw stack, which might be easier than looking for information from a health insurance agency website."

""Right to a healthy life." What does it mean? Did I have a healthy life and how much did I contribute? What is role of society?"

"Latest information is needed for efficiency by which I beat all odds and get trained with latest infrastructure, equipment and facilities."

Ya pressed a button and looked what time it is on his mobile phone. He stood up meaning time to go home. "Good night, Sir," said he. "Good night, Ya. See you tomorrow," said Movan and both departed.

6.

Anyone with good memory is usually unable to forget some of what happened to him in the past. To excuse and pardon people one might like to forget what people did to one. But many times in old age memory apparatus in the brain is weakened and there is loss of memory of events that happened recently or those that took place at other times. Ya does not forget to come to the park. He was already sitting on the bench in the park when Movan walked in through the gate. Ya waved his hand to Movan and smiled. He was happy and eager to learn a few things through discussion today.

"Forgetfulness is a gift," said Ya. "I try to forget gory scenes I saw in the movie."

"When it is a pathological loss of memory," said Movan, "we are unable to choose what we wish to forget and what we wish to ruminate upon. Forgetfulness afflicts every brain as it gets older, thereby losing some or all of technical, mathematical, practical and historical knowledge."

"When I face a personal problem then my mind searches its memory for past examples but I choose only moral and legal answers from among them."

"However much we pray God for daily meals, shelter and clothes, we will not get any of them unless we walk to the store and buy all we need."

"Then we need money to buy them," said Ya.

"We either work or do business in order to earn money."

"My ability to pretend forgetfulness of invectives is inbuilt," said Movan.

"If and when I am punished for my misdeeds I can only blame myself. To avoid committing offence I would study all valid rules and regulations."

"We got to teach students not so much as to pray God as to understand how much hard work is needed to become wise, rich, famous and get recognized in society."

"To develop good character in a child, the one path parents could prevent it from embracing in life is a path of renunciation and detachment."

"Renunciation and detachment are good for peace and tranquility but not for those who have to work for a living and are providers of a family."

"However rich, famous or honoured would a man be, his happiness lies in harmonious running of his household members and close relationships."

"When I am dependent on someone such as my son or daughter, I feel I belong to the family and that way I am strengthening my blood relation."

"I rein in my mind and thus my actions and speech. I know that what I do or say matters very little for people at large. Hail work and words!"

"I am on my own when I begin to earn my livelihood and more so after I lose my parents and guardians. Even more so when I survive my wife."

"Gee! You don't want to live alone. Right?" asked Ya. "We can not make up our mind. Living alone is not the natural thing for humans."

"You are right, Ya," said Movan. "Fortunately it is easy to find a companion. Everyone likes to live in twos and threes."

"Joint families are becoming rare these days."

"Women in joint families are more prone to fight among themselves. Many people want to occupy high offices just because they have opportunity due to their birth in a family of rich and famous people, but not me. For me goodwill is more important than money. Money will not come between me and my relatives, friends, neighbours etc., for goodness' sake."

"For me, like for everybody else, self-respect is important," said Ya. "And also respect of my family, community, region, language, government and Nation."

"Shame can cause depression."

"Do you enjoy a lazy afternoon, Ya?" asked Movan. "Some how I am always busy. I can take a nap but after the nap I can not remain idle. Laziness is not my cup of tea. I got name, fame, facility, friendships, family, and you name it I have it except one thing that gives real happiness: compelling laziness."

"What about holidays?" asked Ya.

"Holidays are not always holy days. If I do not have money or do not want to spend for outings and vacations then holidays are a loss to me. I stay home and get busy with reading and writing."

"Every person who manages to climb up and become the chairman and thus demonstrated his or her capabilities can also manage the task at hand."

"A doctor's life is full of challenges just like in any other profession. But there are opportunities to serve the mankind."

"My eyes mistake a rope for a serpent but my ears recognize the roar of a tiger unmistakably. I sift information and select; yet I often go wrong."

"I am lucky to get help from unexpected quarters but I have to spot the source and encourage it to help me, nay make a fervent appeal for it."

"I have many new ideas and solutions but the risk involved in implementing them has to be borne by me first. Only then will people recognize its importance."

"I do not shut my mind just because I face criticism from close quarters. I regard it as a tool to reshape my pitch to make it more welcome."

"We are wise to store food and other materials for our use as long as they last and as long as we and our children and other relatives live. Animals and birds do not save for the future. They consume on day-to-day basis. A wise man would save his earnings for future requirements."

"The tiger is a very powerful animal but look at its development. Tigers never built a house, reared animals for food, nor raised an army."

"My emotions towards other people, animals, trees, etc., are based on my culture, my upbringing, and my education and not on real harm done."

"All living creatures are dependent on each other for food and comfort. Disease of one is desire of another. Death and destruction as well as repair and restoration are parts of Nature."

"Since I like ALL people to be happy and enjoy the benefits of Modern Science fully, I do not become jealous of my neighbour's affluence."

"Once I gain sympathy of and cordiality with people I come in contact with day to day, it becomes easy for me to live peacefully by myself."

"When I talk to a person who is angry with me, I try not to become angry at his behaviour but try to understand his problem and work it out."

"If I find someone trying to prevent me from doing things that I consider proper then it is only my misfortune that I have to stay away from that someone."

"For success, I depended on my skills, education, information and intelligence but more important I depend on my consistent good habits."

"Emotions of happiness, misery, loss, gain, pride, etc., arise in my mind and I react with word or action that reflect my information/wisdom. But there are always many views of an elephant or for that matter my own personality but all views are of those who see from different spot. So? I never squirm about not being recognized by others as this or that because I feel that recognition should make very little change in my attitude."

"Policy of survival at any cost is the best policy but it fails when I deal with a person who breaks law to win at any cost to herself/himself. We need the help from our community to deal with lawless people."

"Who can deny that a fair-skinned (white) person is more attractive than a dark person? But I like all people who smile and appear friendly."

"While posing for a photograph we are asked to smile. Smile! Some illnesses prevent us from smiling; one such is Parkinson's disease... I am practicing smiling."

"Longer I sleep undisturbed the longer will I be out of the way of others and less would I react to what I see, hear, read, or get a phone call."

"I have realized WHY I remember more of my past misdeeds than any good I did. My initial upbringing taught me what is wrong and what's right."

"I do not jump to conclusions anymore as easily as before because there are chances that my understanding is erroneous and reality different."

"As I grow older the opportunities for me to become useful to the community begin to disappear and donating to charity is all that remains."

"I do not anymore find faults with people doing things around me because I was myself not faultless, not impeccable, not perfect, not on the target, etc."

"Life of every human must be saved," said Ya. "Lives of wild animals also must be saved."

"Lives of grazing animals such as cattle and lives of birds such as cocks and hens as also the lives of fish in the river and sea are expendable. We slaughter them for food but they reproduce themselves easily."

"It is a million times harder to get a living thing such as a human child born but it is so easy to finish one off; shows cheapness of life."

"Most of what might happen next around us is predictable. Fear of tomorrow and of our future is unwarranted for the short span of human life."

"I have wondered if a fatal disease is a relief when it attacks a person who finds living her/his life to be riddled with unsolvable problems."

"A person, ignorant of processes of life/death may commit suicide to achieve a vengeful objective but he won't live to see if he succeeded."

"After reading about living conditions in the past couple of centuries in India, I find that there have been changes in life for the better."

"If I close my mind to new information and thus block new ideas from transforming my ways of life then I am bound to face potholed prospects."

"I don't think I would enjoy things that I didn't work for; but if things are thrown at me for me to enjoy then probably I deserve them fine."

"It is not useful to live a long retired life unless I make use of the retirement to embellish my work and expose my past good and bad deeds."

"I feel the pressure my body exerts on my mind through their own links making me fearful of actions that cause ill will, hurt relations, etc."

"I know that my body and mind go along with the diurnal variations that occur around me all-day and I function better by moving along with it."

"Happiness is the result we look forward to after our hard work," said Ya. "Do we have right to benefits that arise as a result of our work?"

"I feel we have a right to the result and not just work," replied Movan. "The contention of some of our scriptures that we have no right to the fruits of our labour is sheer nonsense. We got to be selfish and look forward to gains after working.".

"Legends and mythological stories direct us to think and do things today the way they narrate but I decide to do it all in the modern way."

"If I have to fight against strong forces for my rights and likely lose the battle then I rather join those forces and gain similar benefits."

"I don't wait for a gigantic opportunity to make it big in life because smaller the cake easier to eat it. Also there are many others waiting."

"I wonder how present world could be called a better place to live in than in the past in view of on-going conflicts, draughts, floods, etc."

"We regularly read the newspapers," said Ya. "The headlines are all written to shock the reader."

"Some of the words and phrases are very incisive," replied Movan. "Everyone has a reason for what one does. Not knowing the reason makes the reader handicapped. I generally don't believe all news stories."

"Our mind, a cloud really to store but not an exhibition hall to show all at once is a wonder."

"My mind is a computer which has many GBs of memory. It gets power from my brain and body and connected to outside by skin, eyes, ears, etc."

"My mind has to imagine and picturize everything except what I see, hear and feel around me like my body, my room, my house and neighbourhood."

"I look like one person but my mind is multifaceted especially showing two persons; one that has animal instincts and the other human morals."

"I did not know for sure that most youth belonging to the present generation are well informed about what constitutes good and bad behaviour."

"When I was born I got added. When I die they will subtract. But the total mass remains the same no matter how many births or deaths occur."

"Economics, Sir, is a difficult subject. Is it not?" asked Ya.

"Economics is as good as Ecology," replied Movan. "Economics is Earth Resources Science and not just money and commerce. I want to think Economics as ABCD of moral living. I was a science student and Economics was distant to me until I read a few books of Economy. Economy reflects nation's resources and moral integrity."

"Sir, are elderly people a burden on society?" asked Ya looking at the face of Movan for his reactions. Movan was a typical elderly person.

"Yes, they are," replied Movan. "Elderly people are an inevitable burden on society. Not all, but many. Pension amounts paid out by governments and corporations, are huge. Gross National Product by elders is very little."

"Welfare benefits must be available to those who deserve them but I would never like to be a beneficiary of welfare handout if I can help it."

"Normally the owners of intellectual property (IP) are reasonable people," said Ya. "They do not knowingly steal IP of others."

"When someone gets award for which many others are eligible, then there is vain jealousy creeping up in me but grapes are sour; aren't they?"

"When I think I am the smartest then a bolt from the blue hits me that there are so many people on earth that consider themselves as smarter."

"I have to get used to properties and values these days, as every single word or phrase I create could be my valuable intellectual property."

"Any public property is not mine and therefore it is not right for me to maintain it. Abolish public ownership and then see how town shines."

"When it comes to maintenance the recurring expenses for it have to be provided, which if I ignore then I am ruining my property on purpose."

"Anything can acquire a sale value if I find a buyer. One who creates a demand for his merchandize will get the best price for even a scrap."

"Necessity incites Invention and I can invent something new only if I keep others' approach out of sight and pursue my own new solution."

"My reach to do anything depends not just on me but on how many do I command and how much is our combined resources, properties, funds, etc."

"My output of work and transmission of ideas and thoughts is consistent with my fragile physique and not my extensive and far-reachable mind."

"Even a rich man needs goods and services made available to him in order to enjoy his wealth," said Ya. "In the shade of a tree both the rich and the poor get similar comfort to their eyes and skin."

"When my wife acts and behaves like the Opposition in Parliament, who can not be dispensed with, then I have to somehow induce her to concur," replied Movan. "

"I did not ask you about your wife," objected Ya. "I have seen husband and wife fighting over money."

"I do not want to forego pleasures and save money for the future," replied Movan. "Men want other men for company. I take my male friends to lunch and spend my money for both of us. For the transport, for food, etc. I do not let my companion spend from his pocket. This style allows me to be free in deciding how much to spend. When I go out with my wife, which I got to do often to keep my wife happy, I have to listen to her preferences."

"I can not be of help to you in your dispute with your wife," said Ya. "By taking sides between you and your wife, I will be only losing my friendship with one or both of you."

"My wife consulted a lawyer, a psychiatrist, an eminent domestic dispute counsellor, and many friends and relatives," said Movan. "But our fights continue on a daily basis. It is all about money that I get as my pension from which more than half remains unspent every month. This surplus is the bone of contention. She wants me to save it and not spend it. She particularly dislikes my practice of giving away money to those belonging to my parents' families. I have compiled the list of recent ancestors of my parents and their descendants. I invite them to celebrate in the memory of my parents once a year."

"Do you ask your relatives to contribute money to celebrate?" asked Ya.

"No. I do not take any money from others," replied Movan. "All the money spent for all activities comes from my pocket alone. I spend my savings for these parties and for gifts I give at the party. I do not overspend. I won't be in debt after the party. My wife hates me for spending for these parties. She would shout at me and stop talking to me for days together. She would make me cook food and wash dishes. I like to cook and I wash dishes because the utensils will be clean. I do not shout back at her and try to remain calm. Occasionally I have raised my hand to punch her face but never actually struck her. I become very angry and depressed and often thought of leaving her and go live somewhere else. I had even considered suicide in order to end this torment."

"Oh, is it so very bad?" asked Ya.

"Yes, it is terrible." Movan became emotional as if he was recalling confrontations with his wife that made him think of taking his own life. "But my wife is my only companion and confidant. She is my only friend. She is my help in need. She will remain with me when I am ill and weak. When I lie down on the bed at home or in the hospital due to injury or ill health she attends to me and gets other work done."

"Did she ever threaten to leave you and go and live elsewhere?" asked Ya.

"No. Never," replied Movan. "The land and house we live in is in her name. I have given all my money to her and she has deposited it in the bank in her name. She has got our daughter nominated as the receiver of her deposits and contents of the locker in the bank after her. I do not make her spend even a paisa for any of our house-hold expenses. I pay the property tax, electricity and water bills, and pay for all purchases we make. All the interest income and the pension she receives for being my wife is deposited in her name. I do not own any other house or sites. I have sold my car recently. I do not own a car or other vehicle."

"One of the ways to be free and enjoy life is not get stuck with own land, house, farm, the immovable. I broke away from root cause of unhappiness."

"Does your wife spend a lot for her own pleasure?" asked Ya and stood up to leave. Movan also got up and both moved towards the park gate. Ya continued. "Does she go shopping and buy dresses and cosmetics, etc.?"

"No. She is the one who makes all the purchases required for us," replied Movan. "She is a spendthrift. She will not spend for sarees or dresses. She is old fashioned in dress and make-up. She will not spend for entertaining her friends. She has no one whom she would call a friend. She does not spend money on others. She keeps account of how much she spent and then collect that amount from me. I give her all the money she asks for without any question. I do not haggle over the expenses. I do not make an issue of spending my money so long as I have money with me."

"I try to harp only on the good and pleasant things my wife does so that I keep myself away from causing horror to avenge the bad and unpleasant."

"I try not to offend any one and do not impose my ideas, thoughts, opinions, etc., on others. But my wife has her own ideas and does not ask for my advice."

They reached the gate and came on the street. They went their own opposite ways. "Good night, Ya."

"Good night, Sir."

7.

"Showmanship without real prowess and overacted, might cause accident and even fatality and therefore I resist myself from performing browbeating acts," said Movan as he settled down on the park bench beside Ya. Ya had come to the park a bit earlier than usual. ""Apart from feeding myself and taking care of my person, I can venture into one or other tasks but I am not eager to accomplish anything special anymore. I have ceased to be ambitious. I only look forward to the curtain-fall."

"No one can predict his or her death," said Ya. "You I guess will live longer than your ancestors did. All the advances in medicine and science has prolonged the life of humans on earth."

"The world is so big and wide but our mind is bigger and wider. Much of what our mind reads about the world is speculation and imagination, "said Movan. " When our parents are gone, we have no one to complain to or hold responsible for our miseries and misfortunes. Instead, I congratulate them and thank them for giving life to me."

"Often we estimate our worth correctly and yet our friends and acquaintances over-rate us," said Ya. "Only our heir will know how valuable we are, after we are gone."

"Yes. What we leave behind may or may not be valuable to our heirs," replied Movan. "My acts of omission and commission determine how the society looks at me. It is up to me to do good things and speak well of folks around me."

"What was said many years ago might not be relevant today. I would first decide if what was said many years ago is applicable today or not."

"I think it is easy to quote from ancient books often incorrectly. I have to work hard and think deeply before I might take them up for help."

"I have to go along with appeals from my mind and body for rest and relaxation because I am part of the Universe and have to follow its laws."

"Information is more than knowledge. Latest information enables us to make decisions. Giving false information is deceit that weakens us."

"Is it only the people or is it also the government that can make life livable?" asked Ya.

"Secure borders of the country and preservation of liberty, language, culture and equality are matters as important as material development," replied Movan. "The world cannot now deny that India is really rich and powerful with the government utilizing the nascent greatness of India."

"Globalization requires India to compete with the world by introducing new currency. The Indian Dollar IND equal to 100 Rupees might become a prestige issue."

"Democracy is somewhere between dictatorship and anarchy. A Republic like India must spend more on governance to keep all her citizens happy."

"I am only one among millions of people on earth, only 5 ft 3 in ht and 68 kg in wt but I pride myself that my mind spans the entire universe."

"Cleanliness is only one means to stop common illnesses. It is not possible for me to order people around to keep their surroundings swatcha and clean like I do. They say, 'mind your own business.' You see?"

"If we put the thought of cleanliness as a means to show patriotism then people don't want to become antinational by littering, spitting, and generally spoiling looks and feel of their neighbourhood, town and country."

"Voter education must include watching if prompt and up-to-date revision of Voter Lists done or not; missing name in the list is loss of Votership."

"At least democracies and elections have surprises in store; allow change sans war and violence, make a minister a pauper, and vice versa, phata phat."

"There is no dearth of intellectuals, scientists, saints, etc. among us but we lack people who consider throwing garbage on streets as a bad habit."

"Talking on the mobile phone while moving in traffic on a vehicle is invitation to cause injury and death to both oneself and to others."

"Like a puppy crossing the road and going under the wheels of a vehicle, the crazy talker on mobile phone is oblivious of danger and death waiting to happen."

"No one taught me that I should stay clear of the traffic on the roads but learnt it myself. I must stay abreast of all Laws and Acts too."

"So is playing with water. Why did wisdom dawn on me and stopped me from getting down into water on the waterfront on that day is not the question. It is the answer."

"What do you do in your spare time, Sir?" asked Ya. "You do not have a job to keep you busy six days a week. You do not watch television very much. You do not go shopping which your wife does for you."

"Yes, I have no job like most young people do. I am now a retired senior person," replied Movan. "I write and publish books. I have written books in Kannada, Konkani, Hindi and English."

"Christianity spread fast in Europe after 400 A.D., because Bible was translated into local languages. English displaced all languages, even Sanskrit, in India."

"Language is man's strongest tool and I want people to know my language but I always try to learn other languages whenever there is a chance."

"Written and printed word is immensely long-lasting than the spoken word unless the latter is also made long-lasting by audio video-recordings."

"I think if anyone wants to help the future generations to make use of his ideas, experience, research findings then he must write them down."

"I am not an aggressor on behalf of my language. Aggressiveness leading to violence is in-built in linguistic fanatics as much as in fanaticism on religion, commune, region, etc. We have got to either face it or stop it."

"If I do not point out the mistakes in what was said or written and instead just praise the good part of the work, then the author would consider me a friend. I do not wish to be on the list of opponents of the author."

"It is not enough to be intelligent unless I know how to explain what I know in easy to understand language or I write it down for posterity. Who will read my books? Hardly anyone. I wrote them and published them and that is enough for me. I might read them if I live long enough."

"We write for the readers. We sing for the listeners. We dance for an audience. We cook for the gourmet. The lucky of us have plenty of them."

"It is difficult to decide what is the truth in many situations. The wealthy and strong people create their own truth. Often I say, 'Mine is Truth'; you say, 'No, mine'; he says, 'No, you both wrong. Mine is.' The Wise says, 'You fight. The winner's becomes Truth.'

"Repeat the slogan at every bend and it will become a hymn. It will become hard to erase. Without a question whether it is true or false all people will sing it."

"I consolidate what I learn by putting it down on paper or in a file in my computer because the subject thereby becomes a hard lasting copy."

"Do you write novels with adult content, Sir?" Ya asked. "For many readers the adult stories provide real entertainment."

"I have written one story with adult content," replied Movan. "But I have marked it on the cover that the novel is for adults only. Novels with 'adult content' may have four letter words and other abusive language."

"We got to keep the books for general readership and children's books clean and free from adult content."

"Do you intend to stand for election, Sir?" asked Ya. "Is it advisable for people older than 70 to stand for electoral office?"

"Now that there is an increase in population, we must give more chance for younger people to get elected."

"I might not ever become a leader since I often find my rivals to have valid reason to claim leadership. I ought to accept him/her as my leader "

"Transparency in governance is double-edged tool. 'Sathyam Brooyath, (Speak truth) Priyam Brooyath (Speak lovely), Na Brooyath Sathyam Apriyam (Do not speak unlovely truth).' No need to show all."

"We should not hesitate to ask for help when we need it," said Ya. "Such as when our heavy trunk is on the high shelf. I know I need help to retrieve my trunk. I request a tall man to reach the top of the shelf."

"And a swimmer to dive in water to help some one about to drown from drowning."

"Death and destruction are sad events but they also create opportunities for the survivors."

"Religions are on the wane. India is a secular country."

"No new law is needed to define Secularism as it is beyond definition and its meaning comes out of its practice."

"Practicing Secularism is a means of adjustment, consequent upon need to overcome disputable issues holding back progress. "

"Man's greatest Invention is God, the easiest Excuse. I would claim that God is responsible for all my overt and covert actions and all that happens to me, by me and around me."

Movan had so many other things to talk about but today he brought a write-up to give to Ya. Ya took the paper in his hand and kept it in his pocket.

"I will read it at leisure," said he.

"Shall we wind up our session now?" Movan asked Ya. Ya looked at the time on his mobile screen and said, "Yes Sir. Thank you, and good night."

"Good night, Ya."

8.

Ya was on the bus. He was eager to read the paper Movan gave him in the park. He took it out from his shirt pocket and began to read it.

"Overindulgence in pleasant things should at the most be limited to once or twice a year; otherwise our body and mind get overworked badly."

"It's not easy for me to find out what gift a recipient is expecting from me. I surprise her/him by presenting one that she/he presumably always wanted."

"Technique and method in surgical treatments differ widely. Success in their application improves as they are tried, practiced and perfected."

"We got our body out of union of our parents' cells who got theirs out of union of their parents and so on. I can go back thousands of years."

".My blood boils when I read about the horrors committed in the past on people, animals, etc. Reservation policy is one way of retribution of some of these horrors."

"If I say I am happy then it is only for civility. How do surveyors decide if I and my people are really happy or not? Which foot ruler did they use?"

"Often it is too late to reverse what I began to accomplish, especially if it concerns materials rather than just skills, talent and acumen."

"Stories of torture abound in world's history. It is unfair to make the descendants of the torturer liable for compensation to be paid for those tortures committed many centuries ago."

"Background information stored in memory about the person I talk to on phone comes to my mind immediately and helps me to control what I say and how I say it."

"The lion roars and so it has to go hunt for food. If the lion were to speak sweet talk then unsuspecting prey might come to him in his den."

"Three years they say are enough to adapt to a new place, neighbourhood, language, etc., and none would blame me for forgetting my past zone."

"The first thing the East India Company did was to open Red Light Areas in the territories they won to keep peace. Do we learn from history?"

"I tremble to imagine what India would be if all essential desk-tops, lap-tops, tablets, mobile phones go weird like my computer did today."

"When I travel with my young friends I got to take a shower and not a bucket bath. Our location is the center of our life for the moment. All we do from here is relative to date and time we do them. We record it for posterity."

"An intelligent person could be a difficult entity to please. Only truth and facts that are scientifically proved will entertain him or her."

"Whatever happens on this earth is limited on account of natural facility. Even our mind can not reach outside nature. Yet many attempts are made."

"We can not determine the capacity of our memory like in a computer disc and neither can I see all the screens in a wide angle view. Is this a matter of capacity or space?"

"I can divert my mind, stop unwelcome thoughts from streaming in and make my mind think good things but can not switch my mind off unless I sleep."

"When I own a property, a car, and I am married with wife and children I will have my hands full of things to do. Maintenance is challenging."

"I watch my beliefs and convictions going through my daily routine to make sure they are worthwhile and change or remove them if fictitious."

"Full stop" is a dot or a vertical line that cuts the sentence off. Death is such a full stop and takes us away lock stock and barrel, truly."

"As years fly by and I get older I scan my life to know if I have been a good man or a bad man. Others might talk good about me out of courtesy."

"No one will complain about a dead person unless that person had committed a number of heinous crimes when the person was alive and powerful."

"To the extent a doctor can treat her own little ailments by herself, she will do it by herself. But if she needs hospitalization then what?"

"We hope that the doctors are life-savers on the beach of ocean of diseases ready to save us from drowning. By chance some succeed! But not all."

"Once an achiever has achieved, an adventurer got what he wanted and the future looks empty then the world looks small and life too short."

"I would not consider protection of my interests more important. I will not ridicule my competitor because ridiculing is against my inherent nature.

"I live inside a big well and know not what lies outside. But I can imagine what lies outside and declare my vision to be true and factual."

"I think everyone needs a companion right from the time one is born. Ideal companion is a woman because a woman can become a valid companion."

"It takes about 2-3 generations for the progeny to be reformed from low to high of habits and character but longer for conscience to change."

"All my beliefs are in my conscience, but make a mistake by thinking that my belief is the truth and came from outside me. Of course, my belief be true or false."

"I do not believe in rebirth or cycles of birth.. Many Hindu Shastras try to tell us how to escape from the cycles of birth so that we do not come back again and again to go through the problems in life."

"Also, I do not think life is something to be avoided, or a curse that makes us go through the travails we face."

"Life is beautiful and anyone would like to live a healthy life for even one hundred years. No one would like to live in a drab and monotonous 'mukthi' place where there is no end to happiness."

"Pleasures all the time might bore us to death. But we can not even die in 'nirvana' to put an end to such boring pleasures."

"There is no such thing as a 'free soul' outside the body. Soul exists only in relation to a healthy body. Our soul dies along with the body when we die."

"Our soul is the life that is transferred from our mother to us as we grow inside her womb. This life is transferred from the mother to the offspring as a continuous action to sustain life on earth. It happens in all the living forms. It is part of the property of nature."

Ya felt enlightened of so much information from his mentor Movan. He folded the paper and put it back in his pocket.

INDEX

12th class, 22
14-yr old, 20
8th class, 19
9th class, 21
accident, 13
act deaf, 38
adult content, 63
Ancient Indians, 40
Animals, 50
Anti-smoking lobby, 32
Ayurveda, 44
Ayush, 44
behaviour, 50
bribes, 11
capitalist, 7
career, 20, 28
caretaker, 3
child labour, 26
cigarette, 33
Cleanliness, 60
companion, 48, 67
conscience, 5
Cost of medical care, 45
Death, 67
Democracy, 60
divine attributes, 44
dropouts, 30
earth, 66
Economics, 54
Education, 17
    Structure of, 18
enjoy life, 58

expenses, 58
fatal disease, 52
female workers, 12
Fire hazard, 33
food habits, 4
forgetfulness, 47
future, 67
giveaway, 41
gods, 15
governance, 63
healthcare, 46
Hindu Shastras, 68
History, 4
honesty, 6
income tax, 13
India, 18
Internet, 42
Konkani, 43
Language, 62
laziness, 49
lifestyle, 3
marriage, 24
Matric, 23
Media, 39
Medicine, 43
memory, 47
mind, 16
mobile phone, 61
money, 40
mothers, 35
mythological stories, 53
newspapers, 53

Overindulgence, 65
personality, 6
politician, 42
prayers, 15
Pre-Vocation Course, 30
quacks, 8
quote, 60
Red Light Areas, 66
Renunciation, 48
retired life, 52
S. S. L. C. (Matric), 23
scholars, 2
school dropouts, 28
School Leaving, 19
science, 5
Secularism, 64
Secure borders, 60
self-punishment, 16
smiling, 51
smoking, 32
Soul, 68
spare time, 61

Spoken law, 31
Success, 65
Sun, 37
survival
    policy of, 51
thoughts, 66
tiger, 50
tobacco, 32
torture, 65
Truth, 62
vested interests, 39
Votership, 61
wealth, 56
Welfare benefits, 55
wife, 36, 56
wild animals, 52
woman, 35
workers, 11
worth, 59
Yajna, 15
Yoga, 3

ABOUT THE AUTHOR

Dr. Mohan G. Shenoy is an Indian citizen living in India. He is a retired Pathologist. He was born in Mangalore, situated on the West Coast of India. He studied in the famous Ganapathy High School in Mangalore and later went to the Ramnarain Ruia College, Matunga, Bombay for further studies. He joined the Grant Medical College of the Bombay University for the medical degree course in 1961 and graduated in 1967. After a brief stint in General Practice in his native town of Mangalore, he left for further studies to Chicago, Illinois, and passed the Pathology Boards in 1975.

Dr. Mohan Shenoy spent over 14 years in the United States in two sojourns, once between 1968 and 1977 and again between 1997 and 2003. He returned to India, and established his private clinical laboratory in Bangalore. Dr. Mohan Shenoy retired from active medical practice in 2003 and began to do things he always wanted to do, such as writing.

Books of Dr. Mohan G. Shenoy

Konkani Books
Radhali Padyaavali;
Secularism;
Amgeli Arthavyavastha;
Hodu ani Sanu (novel);
Hav Daktru Jallom!

Kannada Books
Navadharma;
Innu Nanage Beda (novel).

English Books
Hindu Gentleman and Lady;
Karnaataka Rajyotsava & Other Essays;
Minimum Hinduism Practice;
Adyar Gopal World;
Let's Get On With Our Lives (novel);
Find Yourself Young Man (novel);
The Sense of Vacancy (novel);
What's Wrong, Doctor? (novel);
Bond of Land (fantasy).

Hindi Book
Dharmic Chinthan.

All the books are available online at www.amazon.in